正确的选择

Social Emotional and Multicultural Learning | Non-Fiction Series

Copyright © 2022 by Level Learning, INC. and Washington Yu Ying PCS™
Original and Edited Text Copyright © 2022 by Washington Yu Ying PCS™

All rights reserved. No part of this book in whole or part may be reproduced without written permission from the publisher.

Published by Level Learning, INC.

Content Contributors:
Washington Yu Ying PCS™
Level Learning - Ya-Ching Chang

Illustrations by: Josh Taira

Leveling classification based on Level Learning standard.
For full description, visit www.levellearning.com

ISBN 978-1-64040-084-9
Simplified Chinese Edition

About Level Learning:

Level Learning provides a literacy focused curriculum specifically designed for K-12 Chinese as a Second Language classrooms. Our program offers 20 levels of specific and detailed objectives, leveled texts and passages, mastery-based online assessment, and analytics to enable data-driven instruction. Level Learning reading curriculum for both literature and informational text emphasize grammar and comprehension skills to help teachers develop confident and independent Chinese language readers. The non-fiction series of books are specifically designed to support our informational text course based on multiple national standards. To learn more about our entire offering, visit www.levellearning.com.

About Washington Yu Ying PCS™:

Washington Yu Ying PCS is a Mandarin English dual language immersion International Baccalaureate (IB) World school. Yu Ying's mission is to inspire and prepare young people to create a better world by challenging them to reach their full potential in a nurturing Chinese/English educational environment. Yu Ying's comprehensive IB, dual immersion curriculum equips students with global competencies for success in the real world. As a leader in immersion education, Yu Ying is determined to advance Chinese language programs and global citizenry education by helping other schools create and strengthen their Chinese programs. For more information, email: products@washingtonyuying.org

生活中，我们常常碰到一些选择。什么才是正确的选择呢？

可以问问老师或父母，他们会告诉我们正确的选择。他们不在身边的时候，我们要怎么办呢？多听听别人的意见，自己动脑思考，才能做出正确的选择。

比如说，老师上课检查功课，你发现功课没做完。这时你有两个选择：一个选择是说实话，但是老师可能会生气；另一个选择是说谎，老师可能会相信你。这时你该怎么做呢？

动脑想一想，你选择了说谎，以后别人可能都不会再相信你。这是错误的选择。说实话才是正确的选择。

比如说，你的好朋友不喜欢一个同学。他让你和他一起去欺负那个同学。这时你有两个选择：一个选择是告诉他这样做不对，但是他可能会生气；另一个选择是帮助你的好朋友。

这时，你应该想想这个行为的对错。帮助别人是好事，但是欺负人，就是不对的。我们应该要学会判断对错。

比如说，野餐后，留了一地的垃圾。这时你有两个选择：一个选择是清理干净，但是会花很多时间；另一个选择是直接离开。

爱护环境是每个人的**责任**。从小事做起，爱护我们生活的环境才是正确的选择。

很多事情，都需要经过思考，我们才能做出正确的选择。你学会怎么做出正确的选择了吗？

Glossary

	Pinyin	English Definition
选择	xuǎn zé	to pick, to select
正确	zhèng què	correct, proper
意见	yì jiàn	opinion
动脑	dòng nǎo	to use one's brain
思考	sī kǎo	to reflect, to think
检查	jiǎn chá	to examine
功课	gōng kè	homework
发现	fā xiàn	to realize, to discover
实话	shí huà	truth
生气	shēng qì	angry
说谎	shuō huǎng	to lie
相信	xiāng xìn	to believe
错误	cuò wù	mistake
欺负	qī fu	to bully
行为	xíng wéi	behavior

	Pinyin	English Definition
对	duì	right, correct
错	cuò	wrong
判断	pàn duàn	to judge
比如说	bǐ rú shuō	for example
野餐	yě cān	picnic
留	liú	to leave
垃圾	lā jī	garbage
清理	qīng lǐ	to tidy up
干净	gān jìng	clean
离开	lí kāi	to leave
爱护	ài hù	to treasure, to take care of
环境	huán jìng	environment
责任	zé rèn	responsibility

www.ingramcontent.com/pod-product-compliance
Lightning Source LLC
Chambersburg PA
CBHW041223070526
44584CB00001B/64